Sally

Lehrwerk für den
Englischunterricht ab Klasse 3

Activity Book 3

Erarbeitet von
Martina Bredenbröcker
Jasmin Brune
Daniela Elsner
Barbara Gleich
Stefanie Gleixner-Weyrauch
Simone Gutwerk
Marion Lugauer
Sabine Schwarz
Anke Spangenberg

Unter Beratung von
Jane Brockmann-Fairchild

Portfolio: Nina Winnertz

Illustriert von
Barbara Jung, Wilfried Poll,
Gisela Vogel, Thilo Pustlauk, Anja Boretzki

 Deine **interaktiven Gratis-Übungen** findest du hier:

1. Gehe auf scook.de.
2. Gib den unten stehenden Zugangscode in die Box ein.
3. Hab viel Spaß mit deinen Gratis-Übungen.

Dein Zugangscode auf
www.scook.de

Die Gratis-Übungen können dort
nach Bestätigung der AGB und
Lizenzbedingungen genutzt werden.

pnqek-5kuf2

Oldenbourg Schulbuchverlag, München

Inhalt

Mein Sprachenportfolio
Klasse 3

My name is _____ .

So habe ich
im Englischunterricht gearbeitet:

	1. Halbjahr	2. Halbjahr
Ich habe aufmerksam zugehört.	⬜ ⬜ ⬜	⬜ ⬜ ⬜
Ich habe mich regelmäßig gemeldet.	⬜ ⬜ ⬜	⬜ ⬜ ⬜
Ich habe versucht, neue Wörter genau nachzusprechen.	⬜ ⬜ ⬜	⬜ ⬜ ⬜
Ich habe versucht, in Gesprächen möglichst viel auf Englisch zu sagen.	⬜ ⬜ ⬜	⬜ ⬜ ⬜
Ich habe die Lieder mitgesungen.	⬜ ⬜ ⬜	⬜ ⬜ ⬜
Ich habe mindestens einen Reim gründlich geübt und aufgesagt.	⬜ ⬜ ⬜	⬜ ⬜ ⬜
Ich habe bei den Hörübungen genau zugehört.	⬜ ⬜ ⬜	⬜ ⬜ ⬜
Ich konnte verstehen, was meine Lehrerin / mein Lehrer auf Englisch sagt.	⬜ ⬜ ⬜	⬜ ⬜ ⬜
Ich habe Wörter richtig abgeschrieben.	⬜ ⬜ ⬜	⬜ ⬜ ⬜
Ich konnte schon kleine Texte schreiben.	⬜ ⬜ ⬜	⬜ ⬜ ⬜

Sally 3 Activity Book © 2014 Oldenbourg Schulbuchverlag

Name:

Geburtstag:

Geburtsort:

Geburtsland:

Diese Sprachen kann ich sprechen:

Diese Sprachen kann ich verstehen:

Diese Sprachen lerne ich in der Schule:

Diese Sprachen möchte ich gerne noch lernen:

In diesen Ländern, in denen andere Sprachen gesprochen werden, war ich schon einmal:

So habe ich mich dort verständigt:

Hello

1 ✏ **Diese Wörter kenne ich schon auf Englisch:**

2 ✏ **Ich kenne auch Wörter aus anderen Sprachen:**

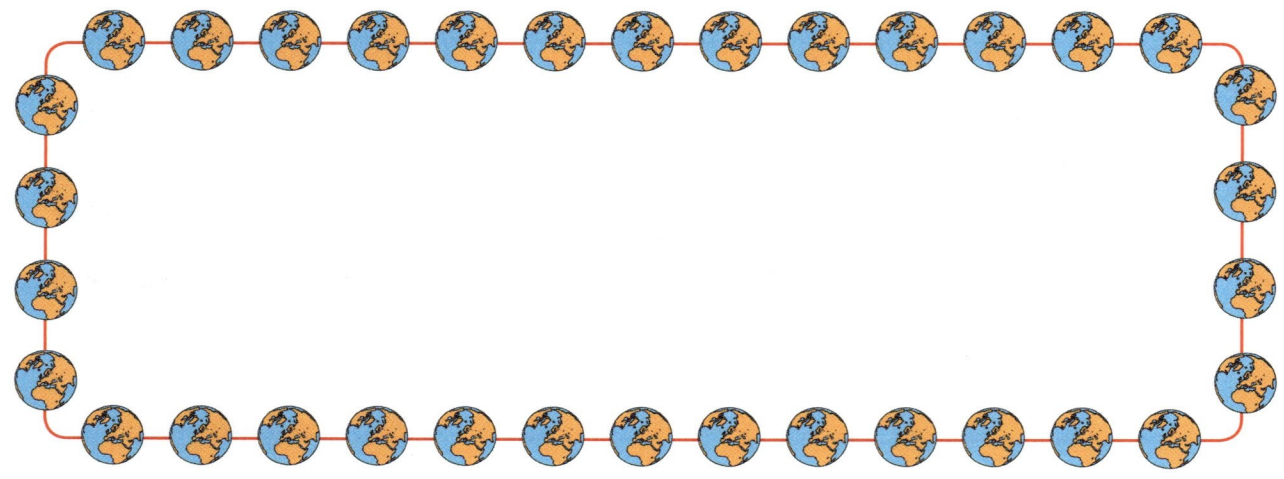

3 **Ich kann mich vorstellen und sagen, was ich mag:**

Hello, _____ .

I like _____ .

4 **Das kann ich auch schon auf Englisch:**

Ich kann sagen, wie es mir geht.

Ich kann andere fragen, wie es ihnen geht.

Sally 3 Activity Book © 2014 Oldenbourg Schulbuchverlag

1  **Diese Farben kann ich benennen und aufschreiben:**

Male die Kleckse in verschiedenen Farben aus.
Hilfe findest du im Activity Book auf Seite 5.

2 **So habe ich „Sally's rhyme" geübt:**

3 **Ich kann meine Telefonnummer auf Englisch nennen:**

What's your telephone number?

My _____ .

4 **Das kann ich auch schon auf Englisch:**

Ich kann andere nach ihrer Telefonnummer fragen.

Ich kann die Nummer verstehen und aufschreiben.

Ich kann von 1 bis 10 zählen.

Ich kann rückwärts von 10 bis 1 zählen.

1 ✎ **Ich kann aufschreiben, was in meiner Schultasche ist:**

Hilfe findest du im Activity Book auf Seite 7.

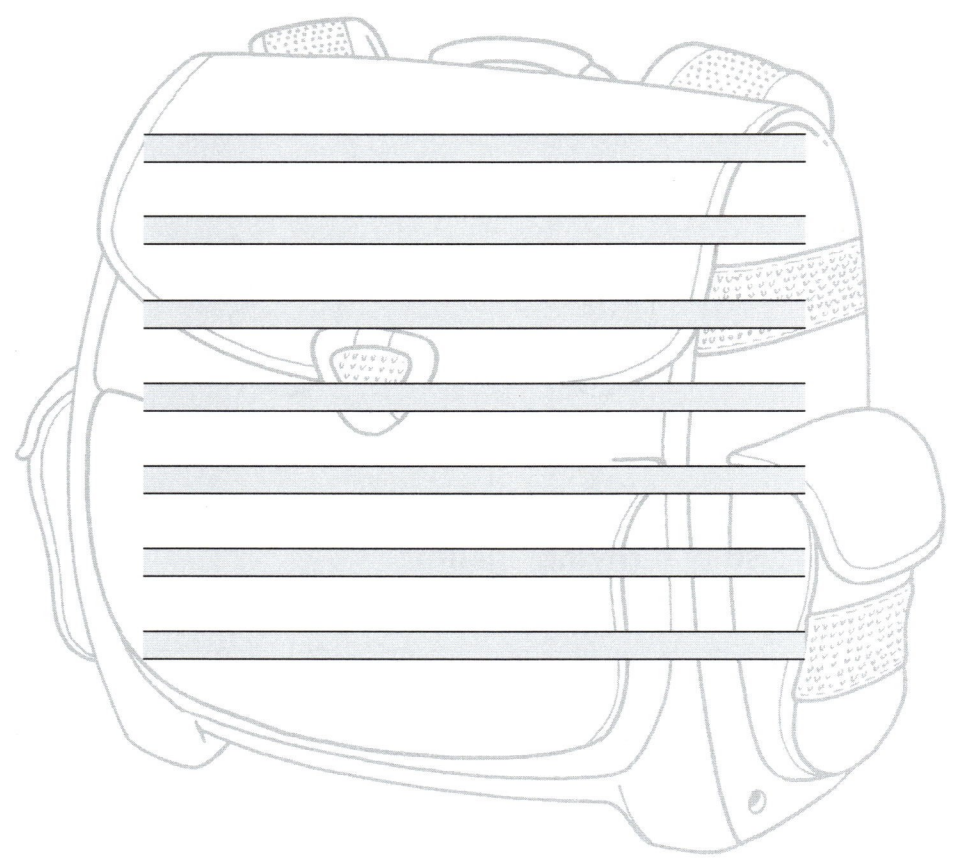

2 **Ich kann die Wörter in, on und under verwenden, um zu sagen, wo etwas ist:** ✔

 ☐ under    ☐ on    ☐ in

3 **Ich kann auf Englisch etwas über meinen Schultag erzählen und aufschreiben (in welche Schule ich gehe usw.):**

I go to _____

I'm in _____

_____

_____

Sally 3 Activity Book © 2014 Oldenbourg Schulbuchverlag

4 ✎ **Das weiß ich jetzt über die Schule in England:**

Hilfe findest du im Pupil's Book auf Seite 9.

5 **Das kann ich auch schon auf Englisch:**

Ich kann den „Schoolbag rap" mitsprechen.

Ich kann die Geschichte „Sally's school things" verstehen.

6 **Feedback**

Das hat mir in dieser Unit am meisten Spaß gemacht:

Das hat mir nicht gefallen:

1  **Diese Körperteile kann ich benennen ✔ und aufschreiben:**

Hilfe findest du im Activity Book auf den Seiten 9 und 10.

☐
_____

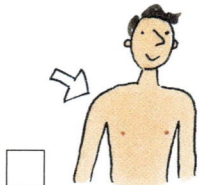

☐
_____

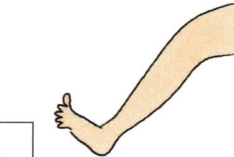

☐
_____

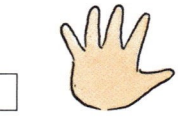

☐
_____

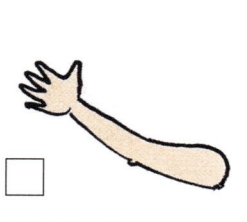

☐
_____

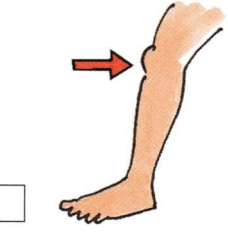

☐
_____

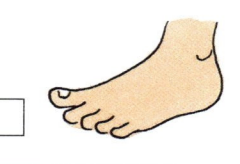

☐
_____

2 **Ich kann sagen, wie ich mich fühle: ✔**

Hilfe findest du im Activity Book auf den Seiten 11 und 12.

☐ I'm tired.

☐ I'm happy.

☐ I'm sad.

☐ I'm angry.

☐ I'm scared.

Sally 3 Activity Book © 2014 Oldenbourg Schulbuchverlag

3 **Das kann ich auch schon auf Englisch:**

Ich kann das Lied „Head and shoulders" singen.

Ich kann den Comic „Ouch!" verstehen und vorspielen.

Ich kann die Geschichte „Get up, Susan!" verstehen
und die Bewegungen machen.

Ich kann sagen, wie ich mich fühle und auch warum.

Ich kann das Lied „If you're happy" singen.

4 ✎ **Ich habe eine eigene Strophe zum Lied „If you're happy"
erfunden und vorgetragen. Das ist meine Strophe:**

If you're _____ and you know it, _____

_____

_____

5 **Feedback**

Das hat mir in dieser Unit am meisten Spaß gemacht:

_____

_____

Das hat mir nicht gefallen:

_____

_____

1 **Ich kann diese Spielzeuge benennen ✔ und aufschreiben:**
Hilfe findest du im Activity Book auf den Seiten 13 und 14.

☐
_____

☐
_____

☐
_____

☐
_____

☐
_____

☐
_____

✎ Ich kenne auch noch diese Spielzeuge:

_____

_____

2 **The fish who could wish**

Das hat mir geholfen, die Geschichte zu verstehen: ✔

☐ Ich habe mir vorgestellt, was in der Geschichte passiert.

☐ Ich habe beim Hören auf Wörter geachtet, die ich schon kenne.

☐ Ich habe mir die Bilder im Pupil's Book angesehen.

☐ Ich habe den Text im Pupil's Book mitgelesen.

☐ _____

Sally 3 Activity Book © 2014 Oldenbourg Schulbuchverlag

3 Numbers

Ich kann auf Englisch bis 20 zählen.

Ich kann auch in Zehnerschritten weiterzählen (30, 40, …).

4 Ich kann fragen und sagen, wie viel etwas kostet:

Hilfe findest du im Pupil's Book auf Seite 15.

How _____ ?

It's _____ .

5 Feedback

Das hat mir in dieser Unit am meisten Spaß gemacht:

_____

_____

_____

_____

Das hat mir nicht gefallen:

_____

_____

_____

_____

Sally 3 Activity Book © 2014 Oldenbourg Schulbuchverlag

 **Clothes**

1 ✎ **Ich kann diese Kleidungsstücke benennen ✓ und aufschreiben:**

Hilfe findest du im Activity Book auf den Seiten 15 und 16.

☐

_____

☐

_____

☐

_____

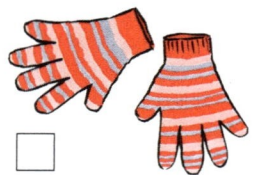

☐

_____

☐

_____

☐

_____

☐

_____

✎ Ich kenne auch noch diese Kleidungsstücke:

_____

_____

2 **Sally in the snow**

Ich kann die Geschichte „Sally in the snow" verstehen.

Ich kann die Sätze den Bildern zuordnen:

Sally puts on her pullover.

Sally puts on her trousers.

Sally is wearing her scarf, her jacket and her gloves.

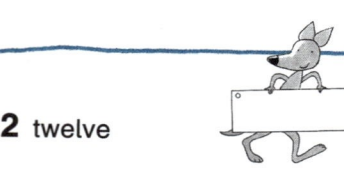

Sally 3 Activity Book © 2014 Oldenbourg Schulbuchverlag

3 🗨✏ **Ich kann sagen und aufschreiben, was ich heute anhabe:**

4 **So merke ich mir neue Wörter:** ✔

☐ Ich stelle mir ein Bild dazu vor.

☐ Ich schreibe mir das Wort auf.

☐ Ich spreche mir das Wort ganz oft vor.

☐ Ich merke mir Sätze, in denen das Wort vorkommt.

☐ _____

5 **That's what I can do**

Hier ist Platz für deine Ideen. Du kannst ein Rätsel erfinden, etwas zum Thema „clothes"
schreiben oder malen, Bilder aus einem Katalog ausschneiden und beschriften usw.

1 ✎ **Ich kann die Wochentage in der richtigen Reihenfolge aufschreiben:** Hilfe findest du im Activity Book auf Seite 17.

_____

_____

2 ✎ **Ich kann mich mit jemandem verabreden:**

Can we meet on _____ ?

No, sorry. I _____ .

And on _____ ?

Yes, great. Let's meet on _____ .

3 💬✎ **Ich kann sagen und aufschreiben, wie das Wetter ist:**
Hilfe findest du im Activity Book auf Seite 19.

In London it's _____ .   In Berlin it's _____ .

In Istanbul it's _____ .   In Rome it's _____ .

4 **Das kann ich auch schon auf Englisch:**

Ich kann eine eigene Wettervorhersage schreiben.

Ich kann die Wettervorhersage vortragen.

Beim Vortragen achte ich auf diese Dinge besonders: ✔

☐ Ich spreche laut und deutlich.

☐ Ich schaue die Zuhörer an.

☐ Ich zeige Bilder.

Sally 3 Activity Book © 2014 Oldenbourg Schulbuchverlag

1 ✎ **Ich kann diese Geburtstagswörter benennen ✓ und aufschreiben:** Hilfe findest du im Activity Book auf Seite 20.

☐

_____

☐

☐

_____

☐

_____

2 ✎ **Ich kann die Monatsnamen in der richtigen Reihenfolge aufschreiben:** Hilfe findest du im Activity Book auf Seite 21.

_____

_____

3 ✎ **Das kann ich auch schon auf Englisch:**

Ich kann jemanden fragen, wann er Geburtstag hat.

When's _____ ?

Ich kann sagen, wann mein Geburtstag ist.

My _____ .

Ich kann jemandem zum Geburtstag gratulieren.

_____ !

Ich kann eine Geburtstagseinladung schreiben.   ◯ ◯ ◯

Ich kann den Reim „Seasons" verstehen und mitsprechen.   ◯ ◯ ◯

1 ✎ **Ich kenne die Wörter für die Personen einer Familie:**
Hilfe findest du im Activity Book auf den Seiten 23 und 24 und im Pupil's Book auf Seite 26.

_____

_____

_____

_____

_____

2 ✎ **Ich kann eine Person (zum Beispiel einen Freund) beschreiben:**

My _____

He/She is _____

He/She has got _____

He/She is wearing _____

_____

3 **Das kann ich auch schon auf Englisch:**

Ich kann andere zu ihrer Familie befragen.

Ich kann sagen, wer zu meiner Familie gehört.

Sally 3 Activity Book © 2014 Oldenbourg Schulbuchverlag

1 ✎ **Ich kann sagen, welche Getränke ich mag und welche nicht:**

I like _____

_____ .

I don't like _____

_____ .

2 ✎ **Ich kenne auch noch diese kalten und heißen Getränke:**

Cold drinks: _____

Hot drinks: _____

Breakfast 🍞☕

1 💬✎ **Ich kann sagen und aufschreiben, was ich gern zum Frühstück esse:** Hilfe findest du im Activity Book auf den Seiten 26 und 27.

_____

_____

2 ✎ **Ich kann mich beim Frühstück verständigen:**

Can _____ , please?

Here _____ .

_____

 **Fruit**

1 💬✏️ **Ich kann sagen und aufschreiben, was in den Obstkörben ist:** Hilfe findest du im Activity Book auf Seite 28.

_____   _____

_____   _____

2 ✏️ **Ich kann ein Eis bestellen:**

Hello, can I help you?

Yes, _____

Here you are. That's £2, please.

_____

3 ✏️ **Ich kann sagen, was mein Lieblingseis ist:**

_____

4 **Das kann ich auch schon auf Englisch:**

Ich kann das Gespräch von Phil und Emily am Eisstand verstehen.

Ich kann den „Ice cream rock" singen.

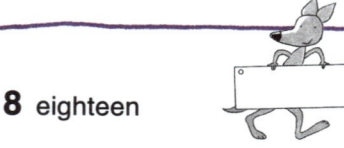

Sally 3 Activity Book © 2014 Oldenbourg Schulbuchverlag

1 ✎ **Diese Tiere kann ich benennen ✔ und aufschreiben:**

Hilfe findest du im Activity Book auf Seite 31.

☐ _____

☐ _____

☐ _____

☐ _____

☐ _____

✎ Ich kenne auch noch diese Haustiere:

_____

_____

2 ✎ **Ich kann ein Haustier beschreiben.**

_____

_____

_____

_____

3 **Das kann ich auch schon auf Englisch:**

Ich kann das Lied „Five little pets" singen.

Ich kann die Geschichte „Little dog lost" verstehen.

○ ○ ○

○ ○ ○

4 **Feedback**

Das hat mir in dieser Unit am meisten Spaß gemacht:

_____

_____

Das hat mir nicht gefallen:

_____

_____

1 ✎ **Ich kann Bilder und Wörter zuordnen:**
Hilfe findest du im Activity Book auf Seite 35.

1	hen
2	horse
3	sheep
4	duck
5	pig
6	goose
7	cow

2 **Das kann ich auch schon auf Englisch:**

Ich kann die Geschichte „Clumsy the dog" verstehen.

Ich kann den „Bingo song" mitsingen.

3 **Animal rally**

Diese Stationen konnte ich gut:

Bei dieser Station brauchte ich Hilfe:

Sally 3 Activity Book © 2014 Oldenbourg Schulbuchverlag

1 ✎ **Diese Dinge kann ich auf Englisch benennen ✔ und aufschreiben:**

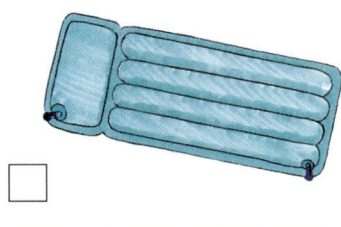

☐

☐

☐

_____

_____

_____

2 ✎ **Ich kann sagen, was die Kinder machen:**

Hilfe findest du im Activity Book auf Seite 36.

Susan is _____ .

Tim is _____ .

Emily is _____ .

3 **Das kann ich auch schon auf Englisch:**

Ich kann den Zungenbrecher „She sells seashells" aufsagen. ○ ○ ○

Ich kann das Lied „Hooray, hooray, it's a holi-holiday" singen. ○ ○ ○

Ich habe eine eigene Strophe zum Gedicht „Dreaming of summer" geschrieben und kann sie vortragen. ○ ○ ○

4 **Das hat mir beim Schreiben der Gedichtstrophe geholfen: ✔**

☐ Ich habe vorher Schreibideen gesammelt.

☐ Ich habe Wörter im Wörterbuch nachgeschlagen.

☐ _____

Sally 3 Activity Book © 2014 Oldenbourg Schulbuchverlag

Hier sammle ich meine Lieblingswörter zu den verschiedenen Themen: Im letzten Feld kannst du eine eigene Überschrift wählen.

Colours and numbers	School
Clothes	**Weather**
Family and friends	**Food and drinks**

Body and feelings

Toys

Seasons and months

Around the year

Animals

Ich kenne mich gut aus und kann die folgenden Fragen beantworten: ✔

Where's Sally from?		
☐ England	AM	
☐ America	ER	
☐ Australia	EN	

Who brings the Easter eggs?		What do you get for Christmas?	
☐ Father Christmas	LG	☐ reindeer	SI
☐ Easter bunny	GL	☐ chimney	EH
☐ Sally	CA	☐ presents	IS

When is Halloween?		What can you say on Halloween?	
☐ on April 5th	HO	☐ Trick or treat!	SG
☐ on Friday	ME	☐ Spooky nights!	GE
☐ on October 31st	HI	☐ Good luck!	SH

Where does the Queen live?		Who stands in front of Buckingham Palace?	
☐ Loch Ness	OR	☐ the guards	A
☐ Buckingham Palace	RE	☐ Tim and Susan	M
☐ Germany	RA	☐ Madame Tussaud	S

What is not in London?

☐ double-decker bus	☐ London Eye	☐ Statue of Liberty
D	P	T

Trage die Buchstaben der richtigen Lösungen hier der Reihe nach ein.

☐☐☐☐☐☐ ☐☐ ☐☐☐☐☐ !

What's your name?

Hello, my name is Sally.

1  **Draw a picture of yourself or stick in a photo.**

Hi, my name is _____.

 **Hello**

Who is it?

1 🔘 **Listen.**

2 ✏️ **Draw lines and write.**

Hi, I'm _____.

I like tennis.

Hello, my name is _____.

I like computer games.

Hi, my name is _____.

I like basketball.

Good morning, I'm _____.

I like my skateboard.

Hello, I'm _____.

I like singing.

Hi, my name is _____.

I like inline skating.

| Susan | Phil | Liz | Eric | Emily | Tim |

3 ✏️ **Fill in your portfolio.**

Hello, I'm Sally and I ❤️ lollipops.

💬 **And you?**
What do you like?

Sally 3 Activity Book © 2014 Oldenbourg Schulbuchverlag

What colour is it?

1 ✗✎ **Colour and write.**

g _ _ _ _ _   o _ _ _ _ _   p _ _ _ _

g _ _ _   p _ _ _ _ _ _   b _ _ _ _ _

purple   brown   green   orange   grey   pink

2 💿✗✎ **Listen to the song and colour. Write the text.**

❀ + ❀ , ❀ + ❀ , ❀ + ❀ . (2 x)

Red and yellow, _____ .

And ❀ + ❀ + ❀ + ❀ .

And _____ .

❀ + ❀ , ❀ + ❀ , ❀ + ❀ .

_____ .

Ten kangaroos

1 ✏ Write and draw lines.

2 💿 ✏ Listen and colour.

seven

ten

one   eight

two   three   six

five   nine

four

> My telephone number is
> _____.

What's your telephone number?

3 💿 ✏ Listen and write.

4 🐕 Make a telephone list. Ask your friends.

⭐ Do you know other important telephone numbers?

5 ✏ Fill in your portfolio.

police …
school …
Grandma …
Mum's mobile …

Sally 3 Activity Book © 2014 Oldenbourg Schulbuchverlag

School things

1 ✏ **Number and write.**

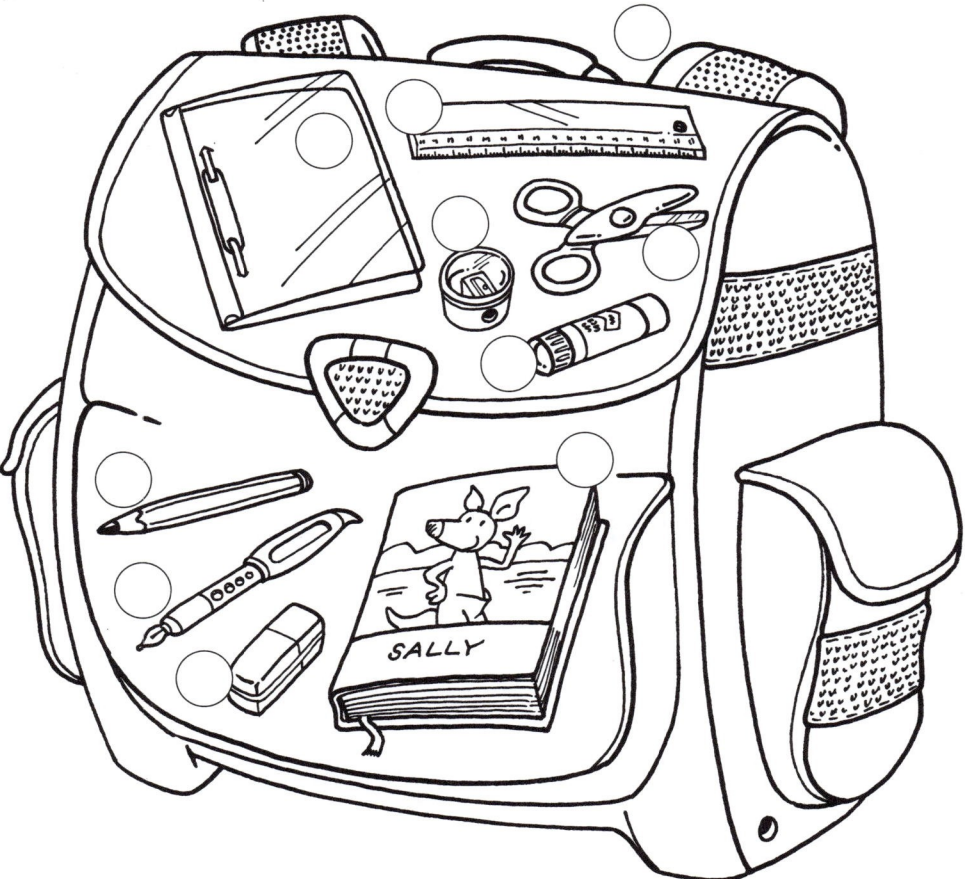

1 ruler

2 folder

3 glue stick

4 scissors

5 pencil sharpener

6 rubber

7 pencil

8 pen

9 book

10 schoolbag

2 ✏ **Colour the pictures.**

3 🧒 **Tell your partner:** My ruler is …

4 ✏ **Do the crossword.**

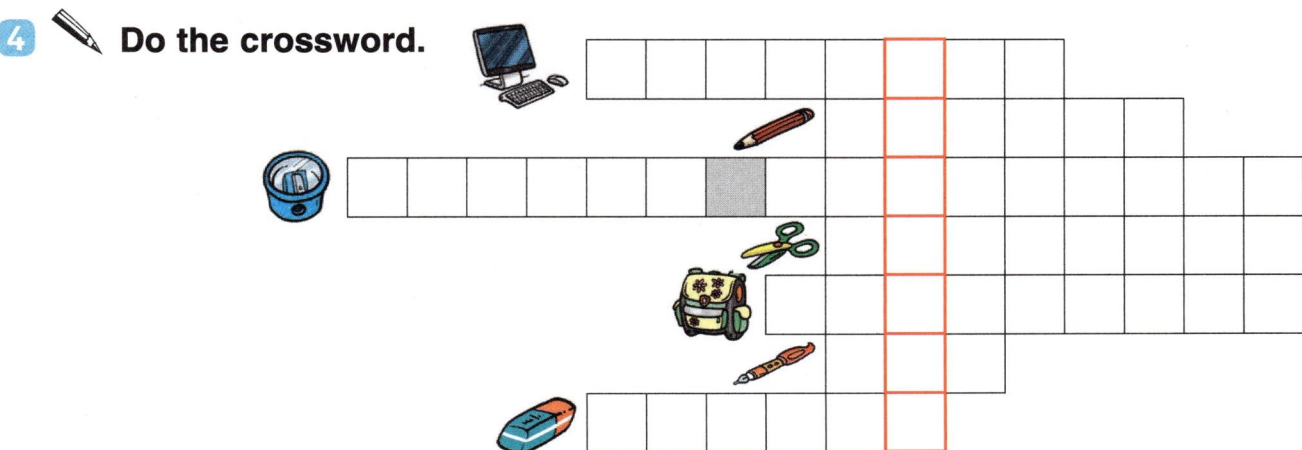

The word is: _____

 **At school**

Where are the school things?

1 ✏ **Draw lines.**

The pencil case is under the schoolbag.

The rubber is in the pencil case.

The glue stick is on the book.

2 ✎ **Read and draw.**

The pencil is on the book.

The ruler is under the folder.

3 ✏ **Look at the pictures and write.**

The book is _____ the schoolbag.

4 ✎✏ **Draw and write.**

5 ✏ **Fill in your portfolio.**

Sally 3 Activity Book © 2014 Oldenbourg Schulbuchverlag

The body

1 ✏ **Number and write.**

○ knees   ○ eyes

○ toes   ○ ears

○ shoulders   ○ head

○ mouth   ○ nose

Ouch!

2 🦘 **Write your own comic. Act it out.**

Good morning, Sally.
Here is your tea.

I can't go to school.

Ouch! My _____
_____ .

Let me see.

Ouch! My _____
_____ .

Let me see.

Go to school.

Get up, Susan!

1 💿 Listen.

2 ✏️ Write the words.

3 ✂️🖍️ Cut out the pictures (page 45), match and stick in.

Stretch your arms.　　Stretch your legs.　　Shake your hands.

Shake your fingers.　　Shake your feet.　　Go into the bathroom.

Wash your face.　　Brush your hair.　　Brush your teeth.

Open your mouth.　　Say: Good morning!

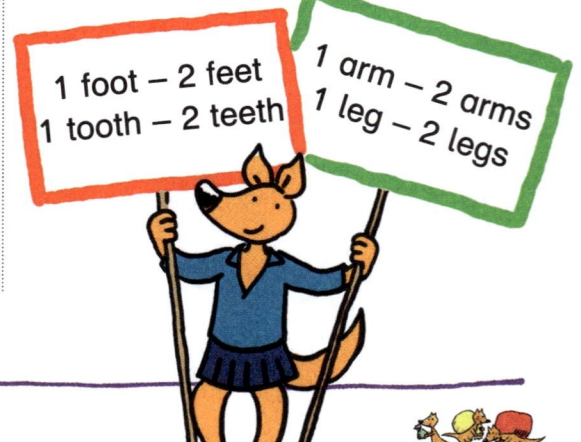

1 foot – 2 feet
1 tooth – 2 teeth

1 arm – 2 arms
1 leg – 2 legs

Sally 3 Activity Book © 2014 Oldenbourg Schulbuchverlag

How do they feel?

1 ✏ **Look and write.**

Phil is _____.

Emily is _____.

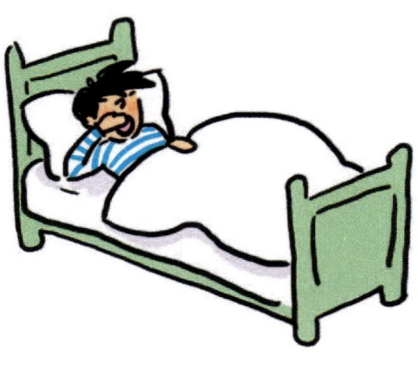

Eric is _____.

Tim is _____.

Susan is _____.

| sad | angry | scared |
| fine | happy | tired | okay |

2 ✏ **How do you feel? Write.**

I'm _____.

And I'm **fine**!

Sally 3 Activity Book © 2014 Oldenbourg Schulbuchverlag

If you're happy

1. If you're hap – py and you know it, clap your hands.

If you're hap – py and you know it, clap your hands.

If you're hap – py and you know it and you real – ly want to show it,

if you're hap – py and you know it, clap your hands.

1 💿 ✏ **Listen and write.**

2 ✏ **Draw lines.**

If you're happy and you know it,

      clap your _____ ...

      stamp your _____ ...

      snap your _____ ...

      say: _____ ...

      do it all ...

3 ✏ **Now it's your turn. Write.**

If you're _____ and you know it,

_____

If you're _____ and you know it,

_____

4 ✏ **Fill in your portfolio.**

sad   scared   angry   tired

The fish who could wish

1  **Listen and tick ✔. Write the words.**

car   castle   computer game   doll
guitar   helicopter   horse   teddy bear

2  **Now it's your turn. What do you wish for? Write or draw.**

What can the children buy?

spaceship £17
helicopter £20
helmet £30
bike £90
helmet £40
bike £100 £200

castle £80
doll £10
racing car £18
football £8
rubber £1
book £5
ruler £2
pencils £3

£10
+£5
+£2
+£2
+£1
=£20

£10
+£2
=£12

£10
+£5
+£1
+£1
+ 50 p
+ 20 p
+ 10 p
+ 10 p
+ 10 p
= £18

1 ✎ **Write.**

	wish	How much is it?	money 🐷	yes/no
Tim		£	£	
Emily		£	£	
Susan		£	£	

2 💬 **Say:** Tim wants … It's … pounds. He has got …

3 ✎ **What do you want? Write.**

I want _____

_____

_____

4 ✎ **Fill in your portfolio.**

Sally 3 Activity Book © 2014 Oldenbourg Schulbuchverlag

Sally in the snow

1 🖊 **Read, write and number.**

○ Sally puts on her scarf.

○ Sally puts on her gloves.

○ Sally puts on her trousers.

○ Sally puts on her woolly hat.

○ Sally puts on her boots.

○ Sally puts on her T-shirt

and her socks.

○ Sally puts on her pullover.

○ Sally puts on her jacket.

2 🖊 **What is Sally wearing? Write.**

Sally is wearing her _____

_____

_____

_____

Sally 3 Activity Book © 2014 Oldenbourg Schulbuchverlag

My clothes

1 ✎ **Match the pictures and the words. Write.**

a pair of trousers   T-shirt   jacket   pullover

a pair of jeans

dress

coat

a pair of shorts

shirt

cap

shoes

skirt

gloves   socks   scarf   woolly hat   boots

2 ✎ **Winter or summer holidays? Pack your suitcase and write.**

For my summer holidays, I pack

For my winter holidays, I pack

_____   _____

_____   _____

_____   _____

_____   _____

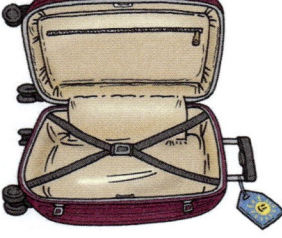

3 ✎ **Fill in your portfolio.**

Sally 3 Activity Book © 2014 Oldenbourg Schulbuchverlag

When can we meet?

1 🔘 ✏️ **When can the children meet? Listen and draw lines.**

Monday   Friday   Saturday

Hi. Let's meet on
_____.
Susan

Wednesday   Tuesday

Thursday   Sunday

2 ✏️ **Write the days in the correct order.**

1 _____   2 _____   3 _____

4 _____   5 _____   6 _____

7 _____

3  **Work in groups. Find out when you can meet.**

name	Mon	Tue	Wed	Thu	Fri	Sat	Sun

Can we meet on Monday/...?

Yes, we can. ✔

○ We can meet on _____.

No, we can't. —

○ We can't meet.

The wind and the sun

1 💿 **Listen.**

2 ✂️🖊️ **Cut out the speech bubbles (page 45), match and stick in.**

What's the weather like?

1 **Listen and write the weather words.**

Hi there. This is Tim from London with the weather forecast. It's another _____ and _____ day. So stay at home.

Good morning from Rome. This is Emily with the weather forecast. It's _____ and _____. Don't forget your suncream.

Hi, this is Susan with the weather forecast from Istanbul. Today it's _____ and very _____. Hold on to your hats.

Good morning, this is Eric from Berlin. Here's the weather forecast. It's _____ and _____. Put on your boots.

cloudy   cold   foggy   hot   rainy   snowy   sunny   windy

2 **Make your own weather forecast. Write.**

_____

_____

_____

3 **Fill in your portfolio.**

Sally 3 Activity Book © 2014 Oldenbourg Schulbuchverlag

Happy birthday

1 ✎ **Read and write.**

2 ✎ **Spot the 8 differences.**

3 ✎ **How old are you?** I'm _____.

When's your birthday? My birthday is in _____.

Sally 3 Activity Book © 2014 Oldenbourg Schulbuchverlag

Seasons and months

1 ✎ Read and write.

2 ✎ Write the correct months under each picture.

In winter

I like the ❄ _____ and ice

and Christmas Day. All this is nice.

December, _____

_____

In _____ I like the flowers,

🥚🥚 _____

and April showers.

_____

_____

In _____ I like Halloween,

the 👻 _____

and witches I have seen.

_____

_____

In _____

I like the ☀ _____,

the holidays and lots of fun!

_____

_____

summer   spring   winter   autumn
sun   ghosts   snow   Easter eggs

May   October   December   January
March   July   August   February   April
June   September   November

3 ✎ Fill in your portfolio.

Family and friends

Best friends

1  Listen and draw lines.

Susan

Tim

Emily

Eric

Phil

Liz

2 Look and write.

Susan's best friend is ‗‗‗‗‗‗‗‗‗‗‗‗‗‗ .

Tim's ‗‗‗‗‗‗‗‗‗‗‗‗‗‗‗‗‗‗‗‗ .

Emily's ‗‗‗‗‗‗‗‗‗‗‗‗‗‗‗‗ .

And who is your best friend? My ‗‗‗‗‗‗‗‗‗‗‗‗‗‗‗‗‗‗ .

Who is it?

He has got short brown hair.
He is wearing a grey cap.

She has got long blond hair.
She is wearing a green pullover.

3 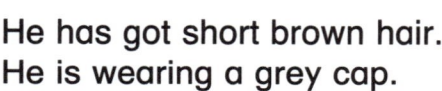 Describe your friend. Write. Talk to your partner.

He/She is a ‗‗‗‗‗‗‗‗‗‗‗ . He/She is ‗‗‗‗‗‗‗‗ years old.

He/She has got ‗‗‗‗‗‗‗‗‗‗ and ‗‗‗‗‗‗‗‗‗‗‗ .

He/She is wearing ‗‗‗‗‗‗‗‗‗‗

and ‗‗‗‗‗‗‗‗‗‗‗‗ .

⭐ **Can you describe other people?**

girl boy blond black red brown blue pink purple orange white green yellow grey hair eyes pullover trousers	 he she

Sally 3 Activity Book © 2014 Oldenbourg Schulbuchverlag

My family

1 ✏ **Find the words.**

motHermumgrandfatherbrotherauntsisterfatheruncleGrandmagrandpa

2 ✏ **Do the crossword.**

3→ ←1

←2

6→

3

(crossword grid with numbers 1, 2, 3, 4, 5, 6)

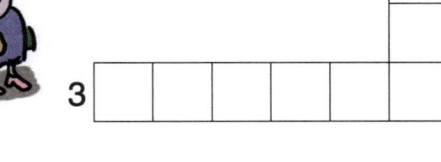
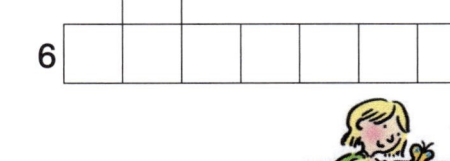

←4

←5

3 💿 ✏ **Listen and point. Fill in the missing words.**

I've got a mother,

a father and a brother.

I've got a ————————— and two —————————.

I haven't got a ————————— or a —————————.

I've got a ————————— and a —————————

and a —————————.

I've got a ————————— and a —————————

and a ————————— and a —————————.

💬 **And you? Have you got brothers or sisters?**

My family tree

1 ✏️✎ **Draw your family. Fill in the names.**

grandma   grandpa   grandma   grandpa

_____ _____   _____ _____

mum   dad

_____ _____

sister(s)   me   brother(s)

_____ _____

2 ✎ I've got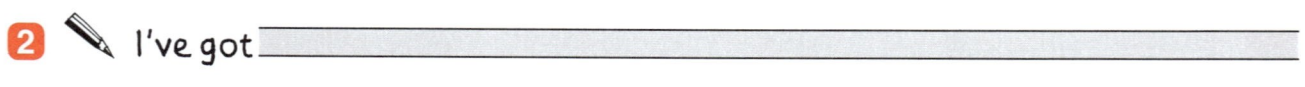

3 💬 **Present your family to your class.**

4 ✎ **Fill in your portfolio.**

Sally 3 Activity Book © 2014 Oldenbourg Schulbuchverlag

My favourite drink

1 ✎ **What can you see in the mirror? Write.**

| water | tea | milk | coke | hot chocolate | coffee | orange juice | lemonade |

2 ✎ **Hot drink or cold drink? Make a list.**

hot   cold

3 ✎ **Read and answer.**

What drinks do you like?   😊 I like _____

_____.

What drink do you like best?   😊😊 I like _____ best.

What drinks don't you like?   ☹ I don't like _____

_____.

4 ✎ **Fill in your portfolio.**

 **Breakfast**

Food and drinks for breakfast

1 ✎ **Draw lines.**

ham   cheese   tea   honey   coffee

milk   toast   jam   bread   orange juice

butter   water   roll   egg   cornflakes

2 ✎ **Find the words.**

honeyrolljam

coffeeteacheese

buttermilkeggwater

breadtoastrollham

cornflakeseggbreadtea

3 ✎ **Food or drink? Fill in.**

food

drinks

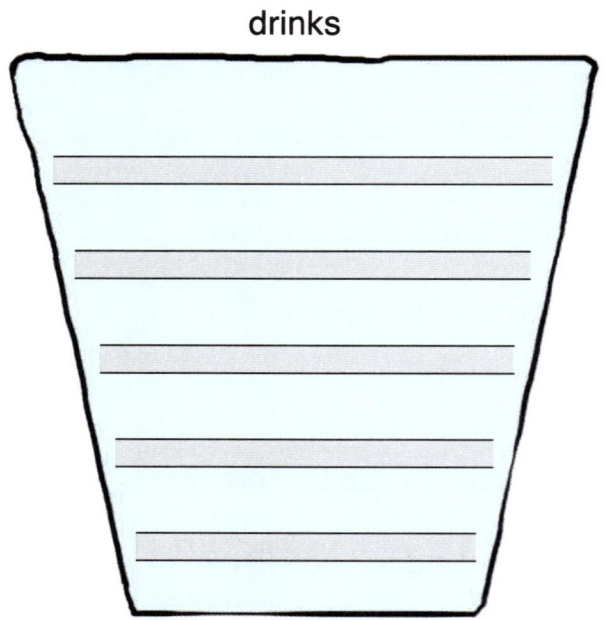

⭐ **Do you know more food or drink words? Tell your partner.**

Sally 3 Activity Book © 2014 Oldenbourg Schulbuchverlag

What do you have for breakfast?

1 ✎ **Look at the children. What do they have for breakfast?**

Eric has _____ and _____ .

Emily has _____
_____
_____ .

Liz has _____ .

2 ✗ ✎ **Fill your plate, your glass and your cup.**

For breakfast, I have

_____
_____
_____ .

3 ✎ **What do the children say?**

I   ?   have   Can   🥛   please   the

Can I have the milk, please?

the   🥣   I   have   Can   please   ?

_____

?   I   the   🧈   Can   please   have

_____

please   ?   Can   have   🍯   I   the

_____

4 ✎ **Fill in your portfolio.**

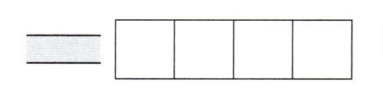

Fruit

Fruit mix

| melon | cherry | pineapple | strawberry |
| plum | orange | banana | apple |

1 ✗✎ **Write and colour.**

a

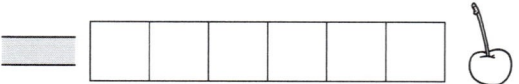

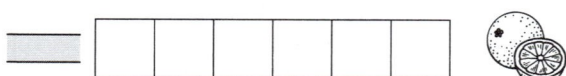

What's missing?
Draw the fruit and write.

It's a _____ .

a **ch**erry – a **b**anana
an apple – **an o**range

2 💿 **Listen and number.**

3 💿✎ **Listen and tick ✔: yes or no?**

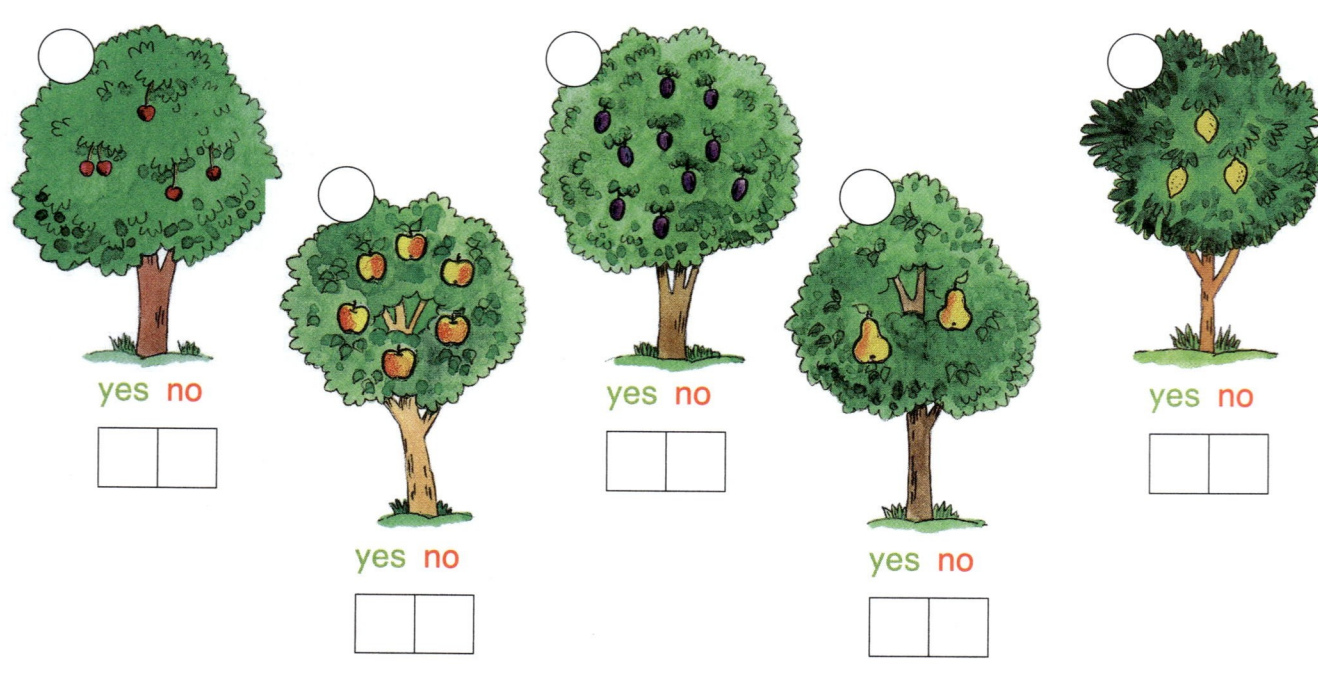

yes no

yes no

yes no

yes no

yes no

At the ice cream stand

1 🔘 ✏️ **What does Emily buy? What does Phil buy?**
Listen and tick ✔.

pear ☐　banana ☐　lemon ☐　strawberry ☐　cherry ☐

pineapple ☐　orange ☐　vanilla ☐　chocolate ☐

2 ✏️ **Fill in the speech bubbles. Act out the dialogue.**

Hello.

_____.
Can I help you?

Yes. I'd like
_____
_____
_____.

Here you are. That's
£ _____, please.

_____.

Thank you. Goodbye.

_____.

3 ✏️✏️ **What would you like? Write and colour.**

I'd like _____.

Ice cream rock

1 🔊 ✏️ **Listen to the song. Look and write.**

I scream,   you scream,   we scream   for   ice   cream. You

scream,   they scream,   we scream   for   ice   cream.

One   scoop   of   or- ange,   one   scoop   of   plum,

one   scoop of   cher-   ry,   one   scoop   of   le-   mon.

One scoop of  _____, one scoop of _____,

one scoop of _____, one scoop of _____.

One scoop of _____, one scoop of _____,

one scoop of _____, one scoop of _____.

| apple | orange | melon | pear | plum | cherry | chocolate |
| | lemon | banana | pineapple | strawberry | vanilla | |

2 ✏️ **Now it's your turn. Write.**

One scoop of _____, one scoop of _____

_____.

3 ✏️ **Fill in your portfolio.**

Our pets

1 ✎ **Do the crossword.**

budgie   cat   dog
fish   guinea pig
hamster   mouse
rabbit

2 ✎ **What's your favourite pet?**

My favourite pet is a

_____ .

Its name is

_____ .

It is _____

_____ .

black   brown   grey
white   big   small …

3 ✎ **Draw your favourite pet.**

 Find more pets in your dictionary.
Describe them to your partner.

Sally 3 Activity Book © 2014 Oldenbourg Schulbuchverlag

Little dog lost

1   Listen.

2   Cut out the speech bubbles (page 45), match and stick in.

CD 2.7

Lost pets

1 ✎ **Read and number.**

cat grey and white green eyes `1`	

rabbit white, red eyes We miss Roger very much! `2`	

tortoise green and brown small head `3`	

two guinea pigs brown and white `4`	

hamster brown and yellow `5`	

budgie blue with a yellow head `6`	

three mice small grey, white and black `7`	

2 ✎ **What's missing? Draw the pets.**

3 ✎ **Read and colour.**

4 ✎ **Fill in your portfolio.**

Sally 3 Activity Book © 2014 Oldenbourg Schulbuchverlag

At Madame Tussaud's

1 💿 ✏️ **Listen and number.**

2 ✏️ **Tick ✔ the correct answer.**

The tickets are	£60.	☐
	£18.	☐
	£20.	☐
Susan loves	Prince William.	☐
	Kate's dress.	☐
	Prince Harry.	☐
Tim wants to see	Schwarzenegger.	☐
	Mozart.	☐
	Johnny Depp.	☐

3 ✏️ **What do you want to see in London?**

I want to see _____.

I want to see Big Ben.

On the farm

1 ✏️ **Look and write.**

one sheep –
two sheep

one goose –
two geese

one hen –
two hens

one cow –
two cows

2 ✏️ **Read and write.** | hen   horse   sheep   duck   pig   goose   cow

These animals lay eggs: _____

This animal gives wool: _____ This animal gives milk: _____

You can ride on this animal: _____ This animal is pink: _____

3 ✏️ **Fill in your portfolio.**

On the beach

1 ✏️ **Trace the lines and write.**

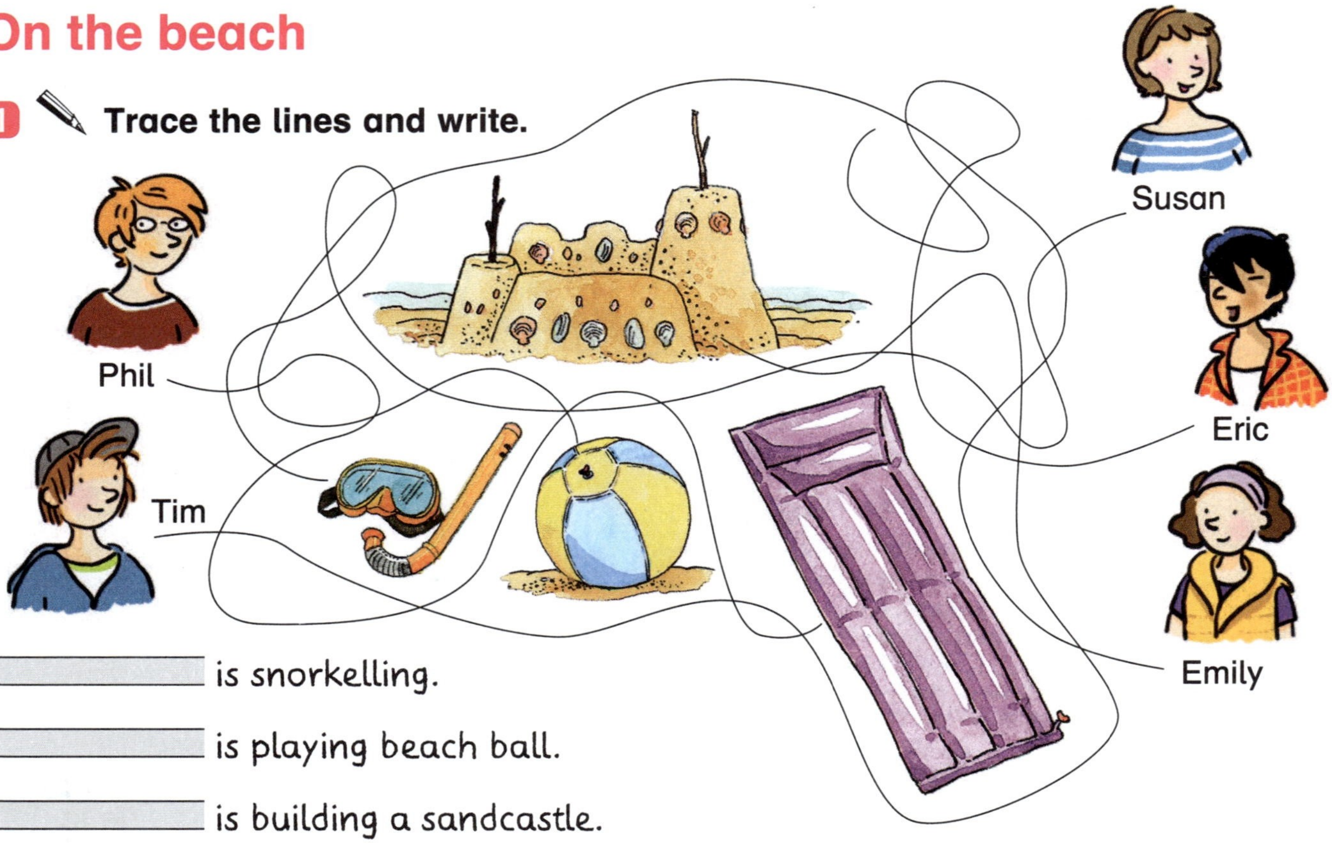

Phil

Tim

Susan

Eric

Emily

_____ is snorkelling.

_____ is playing beach ball.

_____ is building a sandcastle.

_____ is lying on an airbed.   _____ is doing nothing!

2 ✏️ **Find the words.**

sandcastleairbedsnorkellingsummerbeachsunsea

3 ✏️ **Odd one out!**

T-shirt
sunglasses
shorts
scarf

ice cream
Easter egg
beach ball
airbed

school
summer
sea
snorkelling

4 ✏️ **Fill in your portfolio.**

Sally 3 Activity Book © 2014 Oldenbourg Schulbuchverlag

Robin Hood's clever trick

1  Listen.

2 ✂️ ✏️ Cut out the speech bubbles (page 47), match and stick in.

3 🐾 Act out the story.

Sally 3 Activity Book © 2014 Oldenbourg Schulbuchverlag

It's Halloween

1  **Listen and match.**

2  **Listen and circle** ◯ **the parts of the body.**

3  **Find Emily's costume. Listen and tick ✔.**

☐ ☐ ☐ ☐

4  **Draw your own Halloween costume and tell your partner.**

On Halloween,

I'm a _____.

A chubby little snowman

1 Listen.

2 Cut out the rhyme (page 47), find the correct order and stick in.

3 Draw pictures.

4 Learn the rhyme.

Sally 3 Activity Book © 2014 Oldenbourg Schulbuchverlag

Christmas Eve

1 🔘 ✏️ **Listen and number.**

◯ stocking   ◯ presents   ◯ Christmas cards

◯ bed   ◯ reindeer   ◯ Father Christmas

2 ✏️ **Draw lines.**

Christmas tree   chimney   sleigh   present

reindeer   Father Christmas   stocking

3 ✏️ **Now it's your turn!**

Christmas tree, present …

Sally 3 Activity Book © 2014 Oldenbourg Schulbuchverlag

Edgar's Easter eggs

1 🔘✏️ **Listen and number.**

happy ☐

sad ☐

Easter eggs ☐

basket ☐

colour ☐

share ☐

2 ✂️🖍️ **Cut out the speech bubbles (page 47), match and stick in.**

Where are the Easter eggs?

1 ✎ **Hide your eggs. Fill in the words.**

The blue egg is _____ the bush.

The red egg is _____ the fence.

The brown egg is _____ the flower.

The yellow egg is _____ the tree.

The pink egg is _____ the basket.

The purple egg is _____ Edgar.

The green egg is _____ Edgar's mother.

in
on
under
next to
in front of
behind

2 ✎ **Draw and colour the Easter eggs.**

3 👦👧 **Find your partner's Easter eggs.**

Is the blue egg under the bush?

Yes, it is.

No, it isn't.

Sally 3 Activity Book © 2014 Oldenbourg Schulbuchverlag

Make your own board game!

1 ✏ Fill in the speech bubbles.

2 Play the game with your friends.

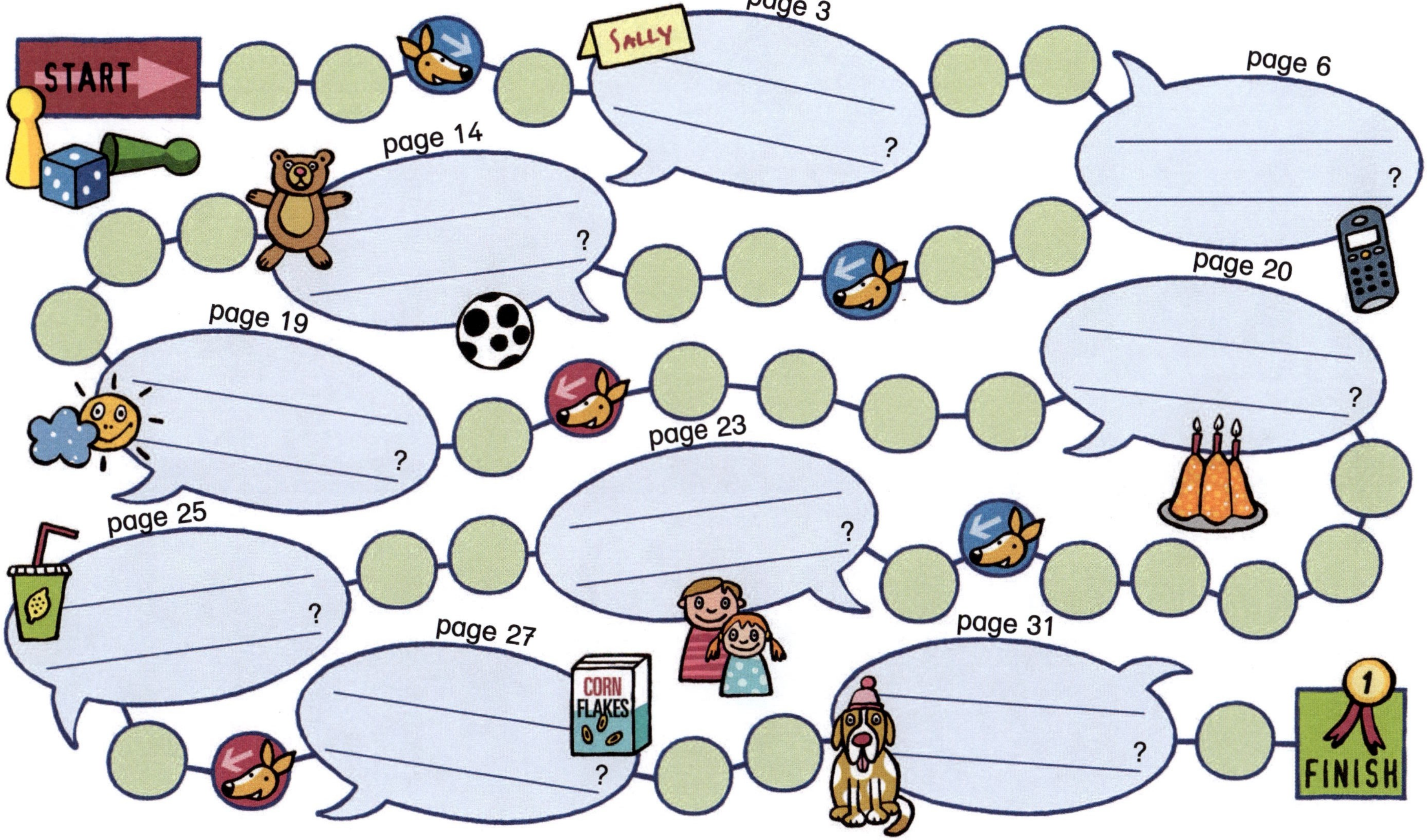

page 6

page 20

page 3

SALLY

page 23

page 31

page 14

page 27

page 19

page 25

START

FINISH

1

CORN FLAKES

✂ Get up, Susan! (page 10)

✂ Little dog lost (page 32)

Let's go to the animal centre.	Mummy, where is Bobby?
Hello. Can I help you?	Thank you very much.
I've got an idea.	I've found a little dog.

✂ The wind and the sun (page 18)

I'm stronger than you.	No, I'm stronger than you.	
See, I'm stronger than you. I'm the strongest!	I can make the man take off his coat. I'm the strongest.	You can never do this. I can make the man take off his coat. I'm the strongest.

Sally 3 Activity Book © 2014 Oldenbourg Schulbuchverlag

✂ Robin Hood's clever trick (page 37)

Thank you, Robin Hood!	Where's my hat?
We must catch Robin Hood.	Oh, great! We want some new clothes.

Help! Help!	I've got some fine new clothes for you.
Hands up!	Good! Now I can play a trick on him.

✂ A chubby little snowman (page 39)

A chubby little has a carrot , along jumps and what do you suppose?

The snowman turns from 😊 to ☹ and Sally knows that this is bad.

That hungry little kangaroo, looking for her lunch, eats the snowman's nose, nibble, nibble, CRUNCH!

Off she jumps and hop, hop, hop, she goes to get a .

✂ Edgar's Easter eggs (page 41)

Thank you, Edgar. You're my best friend.	Beautiful eggs!
Let's colour Easter eggs.	Let's hide the eggs.
No!	But sharing is fun.